My Soul in the Wind

Deborah M. Cofer ♥ Shabrina D. McPherson ♥ Vanessa Jerman Sonya F. Jenkins ♥ Renee Bunn ♥ Ajori Villanueva ♥ Shawdea Carter

No parts of this book should be copied without written permission of the copyright holder.

Copyright © 2019 Joyful Bee Publishing LLC

All rights reserved.

ISBN: 978-0-9996079-1-6

CONTENTS

Pieces of Me 11

Shabrina D. McPherson 12

Making love 15

Picture Perfect 16

Time for Bed 18

What It All Means 20

That's Just How Much I Love You 22

He's My Big "O " 24

The Strongest Drug 26

Further Intimacies 28

From A Cliff 30

Under Personal Attack 32

Teeny Tiny... 34

The Rebel and The Rock Starr 36

Red Is A Metaphor 38

This Thing Called Life 43

Vanessa Santiago Jerman 44

Grow Up and BE! 46

Lost and Found 47

A Mother... 49

Live	51
It Cuts Like A Knife	53
She Doesn't Want to Be Wonder Woman	55
Baby Wings	57
Weak	59
Trust	60
Purposely Made	66
Thoughts of You	69
Poetry from the Heart and Soul	71
Sonya F. Jenkins	72
It's 3:43 In the Morning	76
Love Is . . .	78
Happiness of Life	79
Don't Act Like You Love Me Now	81
Cause You've Changed	82
When I Think of You	84
Time for Goodbye and Hello Again	85
I Need to Know	87
I Had A Dream Last Night	89
Perfect	91
My Heart	92
At the End of The Day	93

My Soul in the Wind

Love Me Now 95
   Wombmanhood 98
Renee Bunn 99
Wholeness of being 101
The Day America Blinked 102
Suspended in Animation… 106
Killing Me Softly 106
Where art thou? 107
Promises, Promises 108
Disheartened 109
Grieve Not 111
   One Youth's Journey 114
Ajori Villanueva 115
Eggs 117
I Remember the Day 119
Great Down Under 121
Regret Letting Go 125
Clouds 127
   Love Thoughts 129
Shawdea Carter 130
With Me 132
She Is Me 133

Growing Through the Headaches, Heartaches, and Heavy Storms of Life 135

Deborah M. Cofer 136

"High-Yellow" ...But A Black Woman – Forever More! 140

Black Man 146

Genuine Love... 150

Joyful Bee Publishing LL C 155

My Soul in the Wind

Pieces of Me

SHABRINA D. MCPHERSON

My Soul in the Wind

Shabrina D. McPherson

Shabrina D. McPherson is a current student studying English Literature; minoring in Film Studies. She works as an Instructor Assistant for Wilkes Community College and for Wilkes County Board of Education as a Substitute Teacher for Grades K-12. She loves Children, she has 14 siblings, 3 nieces and 3 nephews. Writing has always been her passion though she completed a 2-year Culinary Industry program in 2008 and worked as a chef for many years. She is a member of Student Government as President and Phi Theta Kappa International Honor Society as Vice President. She leads an Alzheimer's

My Soul in the Wind

Awareness team called Esther's Legacy. Shabrina has recently begun working for Cooking Matters partnered with Wilkes Community Partnership for Children where they teach working parents to make efficient, easy and healthy meals for young children. Shabrina is an Author/Entrepreneur who runs Shabrina Writes Company; A program she started to Mentor and guide teens who show artistic ability. She raises money to help them follow their dreams and reach their goals. Shabrina can be reached on her Website @ ShabrinaWrites.webs.com.

My Soul in the Wind

My Soul in the Wind

Making Love

It's just like music

It has a steady beat

It sends a rhythm

Through your body

All the way to your feet

You sing A silent tune

Almost like a merry hum

Your heart beats

Faster, Faster

Like an African Drum

Your mind wanders through

Rivers and forests

Like the sound

Of a singing Chorus

The rhythm finally changes

Except it's done silently

As does the end of a song

As it slows down quietly

Yea...It Slows Down Quietly

My Soul in the Wind

Picture Perfect

I love to stare at you
Love to watch you sleep
Love the simple things to do
Having you wake up next to me
So fun to laugh and make you smile
You're always so serious
But I love when you get wild
You go out of your way
To give me everything I need
You are so hardworking
My warrior, you bring me peace
Everyone sees us on social media
They like and comment on our posts
But I could never capture and share the moments
The real ones that mean the most
Like the way you encourage me
And let me lean on you for support
You constantly Remind me
You have my back when I come up short
One thing that I can never regret

My Soul in the Wind

Is Not being Picture Perfect

Because you my lover, have my utmost respect

And the way you love me, I will never forget

My Soul in the Wind

Time for Bed

The lights are off

The Door is Locked.

My toes are warm

The Coffee's Hot

The blanket is on

And my Bra is Off

My pillows are fluffy

The bed feels soft

Opening my book

Near the light for better view

Wondering, where is my nook?

Under the cover with you

My brain is at ease

And sleep is near

Happy thoughts and tease me

As I pretend that you're here

I'm missing you much

With each moment, each day

You are my truest comfort

My Soul in the Wind

In every single way
Drifting off to sleep
The lights from dim to dark
sighing in defeat
I ask God to protect you, my heart

My Soul in the Wind

What It All Means

Loving, Laughing, Baby-making

That's what I can offer you…

Friendship, Smiles, Casual Conversation

That's why I'm here.

Massages, Warm Baths, Moonlit Dinners

With me, they Belong to you.

When you marry me,

You get a wife

Someone to carry the burden

In times of Strife

A supporter on your side

Through this crazy life

If you listen to me,

You get my respect

Make me laugh, be mine

A friendship you won't regret

Keep me safe, keep me warm

Our love will last, no one will forget

As we walk and talk

My Soul in the Wind

We have compatibility

I will bare our children

We will have responsibility

Family outings and reunions

We build community

Mutual friends and coworkers

We'll be in good company

Sharing secrets and a bed

We will have everything

Let us Love God first

And make this our reality

That's what it all means

My Soul in the Wind

That's Just How Much I Love You

It's a cliché to say you're my soulmate
But You are.
Seems so silly to call you my best friend
Let's stay friends forever
Might be repetitious to say you're my world, my everything
Yet, that's how I feel about you.
I was born to tell you I love you
I'm happy to say the words, for always.
Those words are special to me, to us
Just as you are special, and I mean them.
Can't promise I'm gonna live forever,
But our love will never die.
As long as God allows me to breathe,
Every breath I take will be to insure your happiness.
That's so deep and yes, it's quite scary
But we belong together.
God molded us like playdough
and we're a perfect match

My Soul in the Wind

No matter how you reshape us

We will fit, exact.

I love you,

Don't Forget

My Soul in the Wind

He's My Big "O"

Slowly, Steadily, Deeply
Slowly and smoothly
I run my hands on his body
All over his body
I reach every crevice
Its deep, the engravement of his collar bone
    That's where I sink my teeth
Leisurely, Progressively, Severely
Grabbing my hands
Holding them together above my head
Pushing me down softly on this king-sized bed
He kisses me
His kiss makes everything just right
I can tell the both of us will enjoy this night
His lips on mine, it's everlasting
He's in my head and on my mind
His tongue playfully chases mine

Deliberately, Increasingly, Intensely

My Soul in the Wind

He is my Joy

He is Me.

I am He.

I giggle and twist, quietly

He kisses leave my lips but stay on me.

From the side of my neck to my belly

He plays with me

I ache for him

As if I need to give him a better sign

That I desire him

Wave upon wave takes over my body

Slowly, Steadily, Deeply

Here comes the big O and It's him,

Always him

My Soul in the Wind

The Strongest Drug

I am weak

Weak for you I am.

Bright is Dim

Dim, my light is out.

Dancing, I can sway to any beat

Standing up, your smile brings me to my feet

On my feet, I am weak

Powerless, I am starting to feel

Because you make me, me.

I am me, your future bride, your queen

Slave and Master

Student and Teacher

Lover and Friend

Tornado to Small Wind; Unbalanced

Rainstorm and Tear Drops; Unaffected

Marathon to a Stroll; Unbearable

Drought to Dry Spell; Intolerable

Pieces of you to All of me; Unexplainable

Apart from Cocaine, Extasy, Speed

My Soul in the Wind

You are the strongest drug,
The strongest drug indeed.

My Soul in the Wind

Further Intimacies

Tell me your secrets

I'll tell you mine.

I'm in love with your smile

It's one of a kind.

Last night, I tossed and turned.

Turned and tossed all night

The feels I feel with you,

With you, I feel so right.

You laugh, my skin tingles

Lick your lips looking at me, I melt

In your arms

I'm reminded of how true happiness felt

Nervous and shy around you

I'm sometimes unsure of myself

My companion and my friend

My irreplaceable wealth

First date, jokes, stories, Intrigue

Second time around

All fairytale, all make believe

My Soul in the Wind

Pursuing that deeper connection
Further Intimacies
Sitting next to you, years from now
Everything I need

My Soul in the Wind

From A Cliff

The sky is falling

The ground is lifting

No, I'm floating

My thoughts as I ascend

Thoughts as I descend

Into a lifeless world

Into a loveless life

Rocks beneath me rumble

Knees begin to shake

Never thought I survive

My last heartbreak

The pain from that loss

Life falling from a cliff

Like sleeping awkwardly

Waking up, neck Stiff

Catching my breath

Close to separation

Gasping for air

Releasing desperation

My Soul in the Wind

Falling in love again,

Falling to my death

You are what's been missing in my life

Your love is what's Best

Shedding light on what matters most

Thoughts of our love, our reason to boast

I know I'm in love,

He's Special.

My Soul in the Wind

Under Personal Attack

This is Not about you being black
But the Melanin in your Skin is intimidating
This is not a Personal Attack
But your Identity is being Violated
I will no longer Stand Up for her
I won't point out what they do wrong
And not because I don't love my sister
But because they've been mistreating you so long
There will be a moment
A time when you have to face
The ones that are disrespectful
From the ones that "just made a mistake"
This is Not about you being Black
It's about your talent and your drive
This is Not a Personal Attack
It's what you have that money can't buy
I want to scream and shout
Throw hands and go down fighting
I want to flip this world inside out

My Soul in the Wind

And let these flames keep igniting

I won't tell you they are doing you dirty

I will just show you what clean looks like

I will just remind you that you are WORTHY

While you remind me what a Queen is like

This is Not about you being black

But the Melanin in your Skin is intimidating

This is not a Personal Attack

But your Identity is being Violated

For Bella

My Soul in the Wind

Teeny Tiny

The smell of the tops of their head
Babies smell so good
Watching them sleep in bed
They are the light of the world
Ity Bity
Their clothes fit them snug
Small and perfect,
Careful when you give them hugs
Teeny tiny
Their feet barely fill their socks
Constantly on your brain
As you care for them around the clock
It is completely worth it
to watch them learn and grow
Bringing them up to be strong
Teaching them all that you know
They advance, filling your heart daily
Their future so bright so shiny
But then you want to protect them forever

And keep them, Teeny Tin

My Soul in the Wind

The Rebel and The Rock Starr

One of me is sassy
One doesn't care if you know it
Part of me is always happy
But I rebelliously refuse to show it
Stick with me and we will go far
I am a rebel, I am a Rockstarr
There's no one like me, no one on my level
I am a Rockstarr, I am a rebel
You may look at me and judge what you see
But choose your label carefully
I have a soulful spirit
And an adventurous mind
You can't ever predict my heart
It's one of a kind
Stick with me and we will go far
I am a rebel, I am a Rockstarr
There's no one like me, no one on my level
I am a Rockstarr, I am a rebel
I love extremely hard

My Soul in the Wind

And I defend what's mine

If you search everywhere, you'd realize

Friends like me, are hard to find

Stick with me and we will

go far

I am a rebel, I am a Rockstarr

There's no one like me, no one on my level

I am a Rockstarr, I am a rebel

My Soul in the Wind

Red Is A Metaphor

Someone told me Red is my color at the gym today...
I smile & agreed.
I appreciated the compliment because for Years I would've disagreed...
10 years ago, my mom bought me a Red Sweat suit.
it was a short-sleeved hoodie sweat suit and So comfy!
(Thanks Sharon... in case I've never said it!)
And some of my Brothers decided to pick on Me when I put it on...
One said I looked like Mrs. CLAUS (Santa's Wife)
One said I looked like a Giant Red Apple...
and the jokes just Kept coming...
this was how they "played"
To them, it was Just fun.
To me, I looked like Ms. CLAUS AND A GIANT RED APPLE.
I was unable to appreciate the kind gesture my hardworking mother made when she saw this

comfortable red Sweat suit in my size and brought it home to me.

I STOPPED WEARING RED FOR ABOUT 6 YEARS after this...

Fast forward to 2012, I Fall in love with a man who at the time I thought was a fantastic human being, He Loved Red & requested me to wear it... so, I did! And Suddenly I Loved Red again... years go by and just like MOST,

He was an ass, so I doubted my belief that Red ever looked good on me

I HATE RED all over again...

PRESENT DAY. RED IS VERY MUCH A PART OF MY WARDROBE.

and not because of what ANY MAN has to say about it...

Brother. Lover. Friend.

But because I simply want to.

Because I like what I see when this color is on my skin.

Because I Like my skin.

Because I Like Me.

Which Brings Me back to my Original point,

RED IS A METAPHOR.

RED IS CONFIDENCE,

RED IS SECURITY,

RED IS SELF LOVE.

You can call me whatever you want when you see me in red.

It won't change what I see when I see me in RED.

So, it wasn't my brothers' jokes that ruined RED for me,

It was my insecurity that made me Hate the color & ultimately myself.

It wasn't my Loser Ex that made me Lose Faith in How I looked in Red... well, partially because he cheated.

But it was also Me.

I forgot to recognize My VALUE.

MY SELF-WORTH.

*** as Artists, we convey things differently, we take small comments and Hear them much bigger and FEEL them more than they may be intended, be mindful of the things you say to people... Ask yourself, was that even necessary to say in the first place? ***

My Soul in the Wind

This Thing Called Life

VANESSA SANTIAGO JERMAN

My Soul in the Wind

Vanessa Santiago Jerman

Author Vanessa Jerman has always had a passion for writing since the young age of 8 years old. Born and raised in NYC she relocated to Pennsylvania in the spring of 2007. She has written several books and later on started her publishing company Joyful Bee Publishing LLC. Vanessa wants to help as many people as she can turn their dreams of becoming a published author into a reality and at an affordable price.

Facebook @ Author Vanessa Santiago- Jerman **or** email: joyfulbeepublishing@gmail.com

My Soul in the Wind

My Soul in the Wind

Grow Up and BE!

You are not in this alone.

You didn't choose to have this baby alone; you should not have to care for it alone.

It took a man and a woman to create a child, it took a child to create a mother and a father.

Both parents should take on the responsibility, both should put in effort in raising up a child to be the best he/ she can be. A woman should not have to be the one to make sure the father spends time with the child, he should want to. He should make the effort to be in his child's life.

He should show and prove that this is his role as dad, and that he will make every effort to fulfill it.

Mothers stop making excuses for him, allow him to be a man, be a father and be that dad that the child needs.

Many men didn't have their dads growing up, let's not repeat the cycle. Stand up, grow up, and Be!

My Soul in the Wind

Lost and Found

Something about the stillness

Of lying in a tub

Of water

No other sounds

But the ripple of the water

Based on your own

Movement

I am alone

It is calm

I can hear my own breath

Finally

The peace I am seeking

The solitude

The stillness

Ahhhh..........

Yet it doesn't last for long

Eventually it comes to

An end

I must get out

The temperature changes

I must get out

People begging to look for me

I must get out

There is a knock on the door

"GiGi"

I am found. Lol

My Soul in the Wind

A Mother

She is a provider

A protector

The nurturer of her tribe

She wears stripes so bold from being beaten

Not by a fist

But by the weariness of her struggle

Struggle to put food on the table

Struggle to pay the bills

Struggle to guide her kids in the right direction

She is the leader of her tribe

As she is doing this alone

No help along the way

No partner to share the tasks of parenthood

None the less she is a Mother

Through ups and downs

Happiness and grief

She has no outlet

Her tears are her relief

She kneels down

And looks up
For answers to be found
Mostly when she is all alone
When no one is around
She has to be strong
to make it
Even if she has to fake it
Her kids depend on her
She leans on God's word for guidance
She never loses Hope
For her kids she will do anything
She wears her invisible crown religiously
For she knows that she's a queen
And in time her God will
Reveal to her
Her man
Her husband
Her king.
VSJ~

My Soul in the Wind

Live

Never let go

Life is worth holding

Keep it close

Embrace its challenges

And leap for change

Forget what others think

Their thoughts hold no weight

It's measurable only by fools

You know your own heart

Your value is plenty

So, keep on

Press on

Let go only of past judgement

Former mistakes

And strongholds that kept you suppressed.

Live in life's Victory

Revel in Success

What is success?

Whatever it means to you

My Soul in the Wind

Others hold no value
On your notion of success

My Soul in the Wind

It Cuts Like A Knife

When the people you love
The same ones you've given up life for
In turn makes you feel like your replaceable.
Like the love, caring, affection and quality time was just not appreciated at all.
Father forgive them for they know not what they do.
My love is a once in a lifetime love,
I'm unique because I give everything I was not given. I love differently.
Although the time I have given and still give,
The quality care, the late nights, early mornings. The battles I have faced for you and will still face if needed be. All that I do, did and have done, how easily it is forgotten.
When a priceless gem is treated like the hired help, a mere servant. What is done is from the heart, it is not owed, mandatory or for hire.
It is done out of love, because the way my love is set up, I'm gonna make sure my loves are taken care of,

protected and cherished.

So, take the knife out of my back, and really look at all I do, if it was for hire you couldn't afford it. Its value is too great, its quality is like no other, and it's a cut above.

Loving is my gift.

VSJ~

My Soul in the Wind

She Doesn't Want to Be Wonder Woman

Ever felt like the WORLD was on your shoulders?
Like the burden was too heavy?
Like your whole life you've made sacrifice after sacrifice for everyone except yourself?
Ever looked out the window and smiled because the day was so beautiful, and you thought maybe I'll go out to enjoy it?
Then realize that day was for others to enjoy not you.
Ever listened to the birds chirping and wondered what would it be to be able to fly freely, soar among the sky and look down on the lives of others knowing you can go anywhere, at will?
From the outside looking in, we may see that woman who does it all, holds her family together, is there for family and friends, working for someone else or herself, maybe even going to school as well.
She looks to be strong, independent, has it all

together. To us she looks like wonder woman, but she doesn't feel like Wonder Woman. She feels heavy, weighed down, stuck, helpless, she feels like she is struggling to hold it all together. She feels like she is can't breathe, suffocating, holding up that world for others is exhausting, it's overwhelming and it's hard. Who is holding up the world for her? She doesn't want to be Wonder Woman, because in being your Wonder Woman she is losing herself. VSJ~

My Soul in the Wind

Baby Wings

I should never have wings

For I am too small

I should grace the presence of all around me

I should fill the room with love

I should be showered

With love and affection

I should be given the chance to grow

I am a gift

From God the father

And he sent me

Straight to you

tell me why didn't you want me?

Tell me what did I do?

I would have had

10 little fingers

10 little toes

I would have had

Laughter, hugs and kisses

To brighten up your days
But you chose to not love me
And throw my love away
I did have a heartbeat
And I had a connection
To you
Although your love for me
Wasn't there I still loved you!
So instead of innocent eyes
Looking up to you
And me doing baby things
Those who love me cry for me
Because you gave me
Baby Wings

My Soul in the Wind

Weak

My heart beats

My body quivers

My legs get weak

Goose bump shivers

My soul warms up

At the thought of his touch

The passion I feel

It's just too much

Fire burning

Flame roaring

When he is close

Sweats pouring

He has my heart

It has been told

He's won me over

Body and soul

VSJ~

Trust

I am trusting

But many call me naive

I give a chance to those who others say don't deserve it.

My mom says guilty,

Until proven innocent

And that trust is earned

Not given

But I have such a big heart

That just not how I was living

So, I open my heart

I don't put up walls

Allowing trust to be my greatest downfall

Blindly, I let people enter my life

Thinking people

Just can't be that bad

I give the benefit of doubt

Not doing my homework

And finding out what they are

My Soul in the Wind

Really about

So, I allow them to enter

I call them a friend

And I'm the ones whose

Heart is used, abused and walked on in the end

I share my secrets

I confide in them

But they use it for ammunition

Against me

I've loved and I have been there

For others who at times I come to miss

But reality sets in

And I remember

In the end they've given me

Their ass to kiss

So, although trust is broken

And my heart seems

It won't be repaired

I will make it through this

I will be strong again

God will send me good people

He will send me genuine friends

And for my heart

It's a little blue,

It's a little heavy

From trusting you

But I'm strong, because that's how I was made

And in time the hurt will fade

So, for now I am doing me

Focusing on bettering my life

Because No one can love me

Like I love me

and pulling back

Keeps me at bay from

Misery and strife

I am learning lessons

That my momma already

done warned me about

But I guess

It's my downfall

Because I gave the benefit of doubt

Everything is not what it seems

My Soul in the Wind

Everyone is not whom they portray

But I guess that's just the way they are

Some just live to lie and steal

Lie to gain your trust

Live to steal your friendship

Knowing they only have ill intentions

But it's their loss not mine

I will forever be fine

Because I will always have my family

My mother says

Some people are vindictive,

They praise on those who have good hearts

They use, take and save things you've told just to use it against you in the end

Those people are of the devil

Those people aren't your friend

But God will always show you

He will show you who is real

He gives you signs and warnings

But often you choose to overlook them, or give them another chance but a person will always show their true colors

    It's just a matter of time

    Before its revealed

    And the truth comes out when people are mad

    They speak what's on their minds

    So, don't take that as just getting back at you

    That moment is when they are

    Most true.

    Let go of those people,

    Move on and don't look back

    If they mean you no good now

    Trust they will not change

    If they choose to judge you

    For mistakes you have made

    Hold you head high

    And live your life anyway

    Because everyone has their secrets

    They have things that they've done too

    But it pushes their problems to the side

    When they put the focus on you

My Soul in the Wind

People are gonna talk
Whether you're doing good or bad
So, let them go, never let them back into your life
Better days are coming, and your life will be so free
Hear the words that I am speaking
Put your trust in ME!!
   VSJ~

My Soul in the Wind

Purposely Made

On purpose

On purpose I was born

Gods purpose

Before I was conceived

Gods plans was already written

He created me

On purpose

Knowing the road, I would follow

The path was Already chosen

There are no mistakes

For what I thought was a mistake

Was Gods way of showing me

I was off course

I once did mindless things

Ran with the wrong crowd

But I was shown that life

Is about choices

Some lead us to greatness

Some keep us stuck

My Soul in the Wind

And some lead to destruction
When I learned to put away childish
Things
My life began to change
I started to notice
That many are stuck
Stuck in a certain mentality
Stuck in a certain way of life
God showed me the big picture
My vision is clear
The cloudiness has vanished
I have accomplished many things
I am living a well-rounded life
Not according to society
But according to what my Father
Has promised me.
I can do all things
Through Christ
That strengthens me
I hold dear to me
Everyone who is important and

My Soul in the Wind

All things that I am passionate about

My life is dedicated to my creator

Working hard to make him proud

Giving life to my kids, the man God blessed me with as my soulmate, my husband my best friend. I live for them; I would die for them. My life was purposely made.

VSJ~

My Soul in the Wind

Thoughts of You

Blow my mind

Electricity, from the slightest touch

Oh, how I want thee

Impure thoughts

Send me into cosmic quivers

You excite me

Your conversation, level of thought

Stimulates me in ways I cannot explain

Oh, how I want thee

Your embrace touches me in ways

 I dare not say

My Soul in the Wind

Poetry from the Heart and Soul

OF AUTHOR

SONYA F. JENKINS

Sonya F. Jenkins

Sonya Felice Jenkins, former model, former professional singer/songwriter, professional and corporate certified trainer, life coach, mentor, entrepreneur, host of the Internet radio show "Raven's Closet Talk Show," and now a published author.

Stepping from out of the spotlight now going behind the scenes is where she feels the most comfortable. Writing took hold of Sonya in high school and refused to let go, but the creativity and imagination has always been a big part of who she is and how she had been able to adapt and thrive in various industries over her personal and professional life.

Sonya graduated with an associate degree from Essex County College where she made the Dean's list twice before graduating. She is single. Owner of Life's Puzzle Pieces, LLC. and Reaching Prosperity Management. A serious lover of various music/movies/books as well as various television shows, interests in various hobbies and lives in Northern New Jersey.

Author of the following books: Once in A Lifetime Love; Once in A Lifetime Love 2: The Feeling Never Goes Away; Once in A Lifetime Love 3: The Good, The Bad and The Ugly Side of Love {coming soon}. Contributing author in We Rise Above: The Teen Anthology; Rebuilding Your Life Going Forward: An Anthology of Short Stories; As We Lay Without A Care: An Anthology {coming soon} and other blogs/newsletters.

Contact via email: authorsonyafjenkins@gmail.com

Social media: Instagram: @authorsonyafjenkins

Periscope: @authorsonyafjenkins

Twitter: @authorsonyafj

Website: http://sonyafjenkins.wix.com/authorsonyajenkins

My Soul in the Wind

My Soul in the Wind

Its 3:43 In the Morning

It's 3:43 in the morning

A vase I just threw hit the wall

The neighbors are wondering what's wrong with you all

Its 3:43 in the morning

You are in my face trying to plead your case

For what you call an injustice you're about to face

It's 3:43 in the morning

I just couldn't believe my eyes

While my ears are trying not to hear your lies

It's 3:43 in the morning

What possessed your foolish head,

To make you want to bring him into our bed

You must really want me to make you dead

It's 3:43 in the morning

Don't make him hide behind the wall

Didn't you see me throwing both your clothes in the hall

My Soul in the Wind

It's 3:43 in the morning

And because of all of the other times of suspicions I knew

This will be the last time for us cause I'm through

It's 3:43 in the morning

As so I don't catch a case

You can kiss my ass I am out this place

Damn, it' 3:43 in the morning.

My Soul in the Wind

Love Is . . .

Love is something we all feel in our hearts,
Love is a vision we all see in our dreams,
Creating the pathway within to a sacred stream,
Of emotions, too divine to be of not.

Love is how a person acts towards each other.
Giving us forgiveness each day with a brand-new start;
Like a mother to her children and as God is to us all.
Love is pure, honest, patient, kind: it's never hurtful.
It never gives up; handles any and everything; it doesn't sit with the past.
Love inspires, shares, and it can hit your heart fast.
Yet out of all these, remember love is where the heart is, and you cannot have love if there is no heart.

My Soul in the Wind

Happiness of Life

H– is for honesty and respect for others

A– is for the acceptance of your attitude

P– is for your strong strength of trust and patience

P– is for all the priorities you juggle in life

I– is for the inner self you share with those most closet to you

N– is for nurturing your feelings of self as well as for those around you

E – is for all the mixed emotions you feel daily

S– is for self-control, self-love, and self-worth

S– is for all the security you find within and with others.

O– is for the all obstacles to overcome in life

F– is for life's freedom and flexibility.

L – is for all the laughter you hear and share

I – is for your imagination of how you envision life to be

F – is for family and friends you love everyday

E – is for exploring all that life has to offer as you walk your journey to find your life's happiness.

My Soul in the Wind

Don't Act Like You Love Me Now

Don't act like you love me now

Because I'm extra with my civilities and pleasantries

Leaving you feeling like something is going on

To see how our home is no longer a war zone

Don't act like you love me now

When you see I no longer react to your disrespect

Blinded by the fact this woman is fed up and ready to flee

Your friends pointed it out to your dumb ass since your massive ego refuses to see

Don't act like you love me now

For when you get home all of my things will be gone

Yet I'm still here

Don't act like you love me now

See in the morning will mark the date you were set free and no longer awe.

My Soul in the Wind

Cause You've Changed

(90's break-up song)

Remember when you came into my life

We fell in love, it felt so right

My heart never knew, never knew such heights

Those feelings are gone

That's why I'm writing this song

You say it's because you don't feel the same, no more

Whatever happened to those phone calls

Late into the night

To tell me all about

A lover's paradise

Imagine us, watching the sun rise together

I thought our love was forever

But now my dreams are all gone

Lately your kisses aren't the same

Even your hugs are a shame

What makes you want to leave me now

Is it something I said?

My Soul in the Wind

Was it something I did?

Don't you let my heart down, now

(Cause) you've changed

You've changed our love

The gift from up above

Our love isn't the same

It's all because you've changed.

My Soul in the Wind

When I Think of You

When I think of you, I think of our friendship,
Our laughter and wonderful memories
That we are making together.
When I think of you, I make a wish on a shooting star
Wishing that someday you can be all mine.
Sometimes I pray that my wish will come true or
Maybe just a little part of you when I think of you
So many unanswered questions bother my heart but
I refuse to let my dream die but if the time comes and my dream
Doesn't come true well at least I know that we have the laughter
And those wonderful memories of our friendship when I start to think of you again.

My Soul in the Wind

Time for Goodbye and Hello Again

Today you walked out of my life without a warning to find a better life
We could not have in search of another space that doesn't included me.
As time moves on, my life has found something it has been yearning for,
So long without you as my heart begins to feel again it say,
Hello to a brand-new world to explore and goodbye to the long and sad memories of yesterday.
Welcome said the new world I hope you can stay around for a while.
But of course, I can, said I until it's time for goodbye and for me to move on
Let the sands of time heal my heart and mend my wounds and
Give me the courage to live a wonderful life once more.
Today, he walked into my life and my world began

anew.

A new meaning of sharing caring and a whole new way of living

And I am so happy until it's time for goodbye and hello again.

My Soul in the Wind

I Need to Know

(00's R & B love song)

I need to know

When will your love show

Can we continue to grow

Should my heart not follow as you turn away and go

How long will you keep me in so much pain

If you keep going like this, I will surely go insane

I need to know, I got to know

There is something I got to ask

With all that we've been through are we gonna last

There is something I got to know

Was our love affair just for show

How long were you going to be in two places at once

Giving your all to another but not giving me an ounce

There's something I need to say

Before we depart on our separate way

How long were you going to tear us apart

Drowning in emotional sorrow within the heart

My Soul in the Wind

We need to try to bring the light of hope to a space that is dark
I need to know
When will your love show
Can we continue to grow
Should my heart now follow as you turn away and go
I need to know, I got to know
How long will you keep me in so much pain
If you keep going like this, I will surely go insane.

My Soul in the Wind

I Had A Dream Last Night

I had a dream last night

It carried me away

Into another world

A world of never-ending passion

A world of never-ending bliss

With each kiss

Our passions rose higher

With each caress

Our arms reached out to hold on forever

With each moment

Our love consumed each other

Never have I felt such passion

To languish in your arms

To lay my head on your chest

Listen to you breathe

To awake each day

Knowing in my heart

Each night will be the same

Filled with ecstatic love

My Soul in the Wind

Wrapped in each other's arms

My Soul in the Wind

Perfect

When you first said hello to me
When you first smiled at me
When you first called me on the phone

When you first held my hand
When you first said my name
When we first cuddled on the sofa while watching a movie

When we first kissed
When we had our first date
When we first made love,

These are the things that are special and precious
But nothing can compare to the first time you said, "I love you!"
Now that is what I call. . . PERFECT!

My Soul in the Wind

My Heart

My heart is filled with so much love,

The more love it gives out the more heartbreak and pain it feels.

Sometimes, I wonder what it would be like

If my heart didn't have any love.

I think my heart would be so empty and lonely.

The shell would be so cold and hard.

No feelings, no pulse, sadness would be the only thing that flows through it.

How can I live like that, it would be such a non-existence.

Can you ever imagine that?

I can and I've tried but then I realized that my heart stopped beating

And then I died never to return again.

So, I think I will stay the way that I am with

Love, happiness and the occasional pain,

I think my heart can live with.

My Soul in the Wind

At the End of The Day

It is almost that time of the day
When I start to wind down from the daily grind,
A day filled with filing files, making numerous
copies and answering
Telephones and emails
Answering numerous questions, all the while
thinking about you and me

I had visions of you all day long
Thinking about last night and this morning, all the
while hoping for a
Repeat performance.
The lit fireplace, the sweet sounds of the Isley
Brothers and Grover Washington Jr.
While we dine on the potluck leftovers for
nourishment and strength

We lay across the floor trying not to say anything
about our day

But only saying what is important at the moment
We share love that was amazing and so much like
last night that I can't wait
As the clock strikes five p.m., I know what
I have in mind for at the end of the day.

My Soul in the Wind

Love Me Now

(DON'T WAIT 'TIL I'M GONE)

If you were ever going to love me, love now
Baby please tell me while I'm able to know
All our sweet and tender feelings are made from
What are real affections that flow
Love me now, don't wait 'til I'm gone.
Our love is chiseled in stone
Warm words of love that was known
If you ever dream of these words my dear
So why don't you whisper them to me in my ear
Love me now, don't wait 'til I'm gone.
Don't you know what would make me happy?
To hear you say that you want me to be your baby.
If you decide to wait while I am sleeping
Then do it so we can be done weeping
Before the walls of earth come between us
And it will forever be too late to discuss.

If you were ever going to love me, love me now

My Soul in the Wind

Baby, baby please tell me while I'm able to know.
Our love is chiseled into stone
Warm words, your warm words of love that was known
Love me now, love me now don't wait . . . don't you ever
Wait 'til I'm gone . . . forever.

My Soul in the Wind

Wombmanhood

RENEE BUNN

Renee Bunn

Renee Bunn is married, mother of 2 teenagers. Renee has been writing short stories and poetry for over 35 years usually about social injustice or women empowerment. Renee is also a soap artisan and has been making soap and body care products for over 10 years.

My Soul in the Wind

My Soul in the Wind

Wholeness of Being

The beauty of a woman

is not defined by

two breasts, a big butt, thin lips, a wide nose or

straight hair

But by self-awareness

and knowing that she is without limitations

and that she free to be whomever she dares to be

The essence of a woman

is not found in advertised images

But in acceptance of self…

mind, body and soul

The beauty of a woman

is not defined by

her ability to give birth

But by her smile, laughter

and her ability to nurture and love

The essence of a woman

is not found in physical beauty

But in her "interior landscape of power".

               2-27-04- Irene McLean

My Soul in the Wind

The Day America Blinked

I watched TV holding my baby, listening to the morning news,
 talking to my husband as he prepared to go to work.
Dick Oliver-a Fox 5 reporter is saying
 smoke is coming from the World Trade Tower 1.
What could this be? A bomb? Couldn't be.
 A plane? Shouldn't be.
How could a plane veer that far off course?
 then BOOM! Fire... smoke coming from WTC 2
OH my God!!
What are the chances of 2 planes crashing in one day?
 "Terrorism" was the answer my husband gave.
"It couldn't be" my brain thought, "that only happens in make believe on TV."

"Terrorism" my husband said- breaking into my thoughts.
 I held my baby closer, as he held me.

My Soul in the Wind

9:40 am a plane crashes into the pentagon
 This is not a movie.

My sister called from Texas to make sure we were ok.
We are alive but stunned. As she and I talked, and marveled at the catastrophe unfolding,
WTC 2 collapsed before our eyes.
Thousands trapped… dying… dead.
 policemen, firemen gone in an instant.
 trying to help those escape the flames.
They didn't escape the steel beams and concrete.

10:00 am …Pennsylvania
United flight 93 crashes into the ground. So far this didn't fit the currant scenario.
 brave passengers overpowered the hijackers
 and gave their lives to save thousands of others.

10:29 am WTC 1 collapses…
    more screams, more death.

My Soul in the Wind

A black cloud surrounds the west side of Manhattan
and for a moment it all but disappears.
The skyline is forever changed
our spirits are forever changed.

Our government had some of the 19 hijackers on a
watch list.
Well, I want to know,
Who was watching the watch list?
How could we knowingly
let known associates and relatives of the leaders of
terrorism
live here, work here
train to fly planes here,
own businesses here, own property here.
And use our money against us.

America blinked
and terrorism walked in.
We were watching from space,
while the war was being planned on the ground.

My Soul in the Wind

And no one was watching the watch list.

Renee Crummell
9-22-01

My Soul in the Wind

Suspended in Animation...

The Aftermath of KATRINA
(A collection of four poems)

Killing Me Softly

you will shoot me because
   I need water
   my government your message is clear
you will shoot me because
  my child needs food
  my country your message is clear
you will shoot me because
  my neighbor needs medicine
  my society your message is clear

Where art thou?

With no food we are dying
 With no water we are dying
  With no medicine we are dying
   With no shelter we are dying
Where art thou?
 With no money we are dying
  With no help we are dying
  With no relief we are dying
   With no way out we are dead
Where art thou?

My Soul in the Wind

Promises, Promises

you promised me equality
  I received bigotry
 you promised me emancipation
  I received oppression
you promised me inclusion
  I received isolation
you promised me quality of life

Renee Villanueva
9-1-05

My Soul in the Wind

Disheartened

You sent my son away
In the name of democracy
 I need him back.

You sent my daughter away
In the name of democracy
 I need her back.

 You sent my husband away
In the name of democracy
 I need him back.

You sent my wife away
In the name of democracy
 I need her back.

You sent my father away
In the name of democracy
 I need him back.

You sent my mother away
In the name of democracy
 I need her back.

You gave my freedom away
In the name of freedom
 I want it back.

My Soul in the Wind

You sent my money away
In the name of humanity
 Where is my humanity?

 You took my trust away

Renee Crummell

My Soul in the Wind

Grieve Not

We think of Life as a beginning
and it is.
It is the beginning of the hope, of faith.
Grieve not for the spirit lives on.

We think of Death as an ending
and it is.
It is the ending of physical life on earth.
Grieve not for the spirit lives on.

We think forever is forever
and it is.
It is all the tomorrows whispered into the wind.
Grieve not for the spirit lives on.

We think letting go is easy
but it isn't.
It is memories of our loved ones etched in stone
and planted in the garden of our heart.

My Soul in the Wind

Grieve not for the spirit lives on.

Grieve not for those who are no longer with us,
but celebrate that they lived.

Life is a gift and memories are a blessing.
Our existence on this earth is only for an instant.
Grieve not for the spirit lives on.

Renee Crummell

My Soul in the Wind

One Youth's Journey

AJORI VILLANUEVA

My Soul in the Wind

Ajori Villanueva

Ajori Villanueva is a graduating high school senior with the intent to attend Goldey-Beacom College as an incoming freshman. She likes to sleep, watch Netflix, listen to music, then repeats. She is working on a book of short stories to be published in the future. She hopes you enjoy her excerpts.

My Soul in the Wind

My Soul in the Wind

Eggs

Brown and White

Yellow and White

Colors of an egg

hens eat the same food

drink the same water

play in the same coop

Hens lay different color eggs

brown, white, speckled

Different yet the same

brown, white, speckled

Yellow yolk

egg white

Different outside same inside

Like hens...birds of a feather

My Soul in the Wind

Get the picture? Get the connection?

so, what is it so hard to understand?

Ajori Villanueva

1-27 -2019

My Soul in the Wind

I Remember the Day

I remember the day like it was yesterday. I took a secret tour through a park, the most beautiful place I've ever seen.

The birds were flying. The sun was shining just right onto the trees. The clouds were a purplish pink.

This place was sacred. The Indians kept it a secret from other nations. who wanted their land?

I found this most beautiful spot. I read a sign and it said, "Scared ground...No photos please." The wind whispered to me and it said, "Take a photo."

The sun was shining even brighter. The birds flew higher and higher. The clouds departed, exposing God's creation to the world.

I held my camera to my face as I watched the sun say goodbye. Its warmth held me as I held the button. I heard the faint sounds of "click" "click" "click" through the quietness

The sensation felt amazing; I felt so light and free. I heard a whisper behind me, "I couldn't help myself either. It's so lovely." and then I saw her a woman taking her camera off her face.

I stood in total amazement. Here was the most beautiful creature I've ever seen. She wore the ceremonial clothing of an Indian princess. Her long black braided hair hung down her back. Her skin kissed by the sun.

I had to capture this unbelievable moment. Her ethereal beauty standing in front of me. I will never let her go.

My Soul in the Wind

Great Down Under

I travel on this road, alone and afraid.
The floor is trapped with the souls that let a needle filled with unholy sin touch their veins.
The cries. The cries are what I can't get out of my head.
The pain. The pain they make me grieve.
The walls stained dark as the devil's soul.
No light at the end of the tunnel.
I must go on.
I get to that foul-smelling place.
The zombie creatures lurk among the hot lava pathways.
Forever forced to look upon the ground.
Their sin: never looked up towards greatness.
They catch fire when they try to repent their sin.
The human centipedes feed on the burning flesh.
I push my way through.
People are tied down to spiked chairs
Because they never admitted what they did behind

people's backs.
Never told the truth.
Eyes forced open to watch their sins play on a screen in front of them.
The blood-filled tears run down their faces…collected by the blood thirsty demon dogs below.
I can't do this!
The last of my journey before meeting the ruler was filled with terror.
No words could explain what I saw.
An eye for eye, a blow for a blow…you reap what you sow. In the court of accountability, they were judged.
Found guilty they were mandated the to an ungodly supermax.
Punishment: eternal damnation to be treated as they treated others.
I saw women being slashed with great metal tools because they killed their unborn babies.
Men were whipped with a cat of nine tails and

thrown around like ragdolls for the everlasting blows that they delivered to their children or wives.

Cops shot with a hail of bullets; wounds closed, and they were forced to pick them up and give them back. Only to repeat like Groundhog Day.

Their sin: shot and unarmed person of color in "self-defense."

Replay rewind the processes went over and over like Prometheus.

The blood, tears, sweat; my heart couldn't take it.

I must get out of here!

There it is.

The ruler of them all.

The one who sinned the most.

America.

This magnificent creature stands taller than the Empire State building.

It can't move.

It's stuck in a grand box filled with mirrors.

It must look at itself day in and day out.

Realize what it has done to cause its suffering for

eternity.
Shaped as a sphere larger than Jupiter.
Filled with TVs, social media, celebrities, food, vehicles, everything.
A crown stands on top of its head
Containing all its sins within it.
I dare not ask anything upon it.
I simply walk on and continue my journey through the Great Down Under.
I wished I never sinned.

My Soul in the Wind

Regret Letting Go

I saw her

Sitting there, in our favorite spot at the cafe.

We laughed together

Enjoyed listening to each other's words.

I wish I never let her go

I saw her

Looking out at the ocean.

The waves saying hello

We used to sit, in that very spot and watch the sun

say goodbye.

I wish I never let her go

I wish that I said

something

Before she walked out that door.

I wish I could hold her

One last time

I wish I never let her go

Now I see her

Sitting in that spot.

With her new husband and kids

That very spot, watching the sun saying goodbye.

Now I regret letting her go

Clouds

Oh, how the clouds rise

Disperse

Lighten after the storm.

Splashes of purple

Pink

Orange

Yellow

Paint this blank canvas we all dawn upon.

Flight

Awakening

I feel when my soul glides across the cool breeze.

In this moment, my love

I find the true meaning of bliss.

My Soul in the Wind

Love Thoughts

SHAWDEA CARTER

Shawdea Carter

Shawdea was raised in New York and Charlotte, NC graduated high school in 2002, moved to Kuwait in 2005 with her family and started working as a Civilian Contractor. She enjoys cooking and trying new dishes. She loves to travel and learn about different cultures.

My Soul in the Wind

My Soul in the Wind

With Me

Will you share your heart with me?
Open up and be free with me?
Will you ride with me,
For eternity across the endless sea?
All this love I would give for free,
Just to have you here with me.
Will you look past my flaws?
I promise it's not much at all.
Will you walk hand and hand with me,
for the whole world to see?
And say this is where I want to be.
Will you share your heart with me?
Can I keep it for eternity?

My Soul in the Wind

She Is Me...

I would dream of nights like this.

Waking up to the pain I caused in me,

not giving enough love for me or who I should be but who they want me to be.

Who is she?

She is me.

Not finding love in you

because you don't love you.

You're stuck in limbo

To afraid to let me go and find a way out.

Am I still dreaming or is this real?

The pain is real, my fears and tears are real, but why am I did not awake.

Dreaming of better days but wake up in pain.

I finally wake up and the darkness is gone, light is found.

I am loved, I found love in me.

Who is she? She is me.

My Soul in the Wind

My Soul in the Wind

Growing Through the Headaches, Heartaches, and Heavy Storms of Life

WITH…

DEBORAH M. COFER

My Soul in the Wind

Deborah M. Cofer

Deborah M. Cofer, affectionately called "Mama C" by many is a mother, grandmother and woman who wears many hats. She is the author of five self-published books and founder of Sistah Chat Radio, LLC. She is a community advocate, women's empowerment specialist, designer of wellness programs for women, emotional fitness trainer, member of the National Council of Negro Women

(NCNW), a member of the National Association for the Advancement of Colored People (NAACP), and most recently became a member of the Pocono Chapter of Toastmasters International. She is also a member of AARP's Pocono local chapter, a mentor to women of all ages around the country and role model to many. Deborah is also Founder and co-host of Sistah Chat Radio that airs at the Sherman Showcase in Stroudsburg, PA. She also mentors women who, like her, are incest and rape survivors. Most recently she created an empowering Facebook group Embrace the VOW, a God-centered emotional intelligence enhancement program designed to inspire and encourage members to grow and evolve to their highest level of human development.

Prior to relocating to East Stroudsburg, PA in 2006, Deborah was the Director of the Women's Health Education and Resource Network at North General Hospital in New York City, a program she designed, developed and delivered to the Harlem community, where she received numerous awards and recognition for her work, including the Susan B. Anthony Award from City Hall. She has been featured in numerous media venues, including NBC Nightly News, The McCreary Report on Fox Five in New York and Essence Magazine. Deborah is also the recipient of the Pocono Film Festival's Advocate for a Better America Award, the Monroe County Image Award's Community Advocacy Award, The African American Network's Woman of Distinction Award for Sistah Chat and the Monroe County Image Award's Media Excellence Award.

Deborah Cofer has a Bachelor of Science Degree in Community Health from St. Joseph College in Brooklyn, New York and currently resides in East Stroudsburg, PA. where she is helping her daughter to raise her four grandchildren.

My Soul in the Wind

My Soul in the Wind

"High-Yellow"...But A Black Woman - Forever More!

I am often referred to as a "high-yellow" Black Woman - not considered Black or White, neither wrong nor right, just a little too light. But, nonetheless…

I am a Black Woman…standing tall and proud and regardless to slavery's satanic stigma I'm poised and ready to shout it loud.

I am a Black Woman…regal and "real" and even God knows it's time for the world to know just how I feel.

I am a Black Woman…deep inside and just because of my complexion I will not hide; nor will I retreat and accept defeat from those who choose to see me only as a piece of meat.

I will not be used and abused by those who refuse to see. And I will not allow a pervasive mentality to strip the love for my people away from me.

All of my life I've been called anything but – "high-yellow, albino, red bone, White girl, and even mutt." For years slavery's satanic hand has been picking ever so slowly at my gut. Secular words and actions have always confused, but never again will God allow my heart to be battered and bruised.

I am a Black Woman…not just a mindless trophy or a good-for-nothing whore. I am, and will forever be, a symbol of God's enduring beauty now and forever more.

God has helped me to accept that I am powerless to change that which surrounds and abounds within shattered hearts and heads. So, I will no longer allow myself to fall prey to those who choose to lay dormant in bigotry's satanic bed…for I am a Black Woman – born and breed.

I am a Black Woman…who will live and die choosing to soar ever so high. And while - because of a few, I have openly cried…I refuse to succumb to bigotry's insidious flu or live my life feeling solemn and blue.

And no matter what anyone else chooses to say or do, I will not become a member of the Devil's worldwide wrecking crew.

I am a Black Woman…standing ever so tall and never again will I take another fall – just because there are those who feel my ethnicity is their call.

Live in peace if you think you can, but I will not join Satan's marching band or become a downtrodden victim of someone else's forsaken hand.

My heart is wounded but "still I rise," like a phoenix, out of both the Winter and Summer of this modern-day world's ever-growing tide of perpetual discontent.

Yes, Maya I too, now, know why caged birds sing. But, like you, I will not wear someone else's satanic wedding ring.

I am a Black Woman…who's finally free because of the love God's instilled in me. So, a Black Woman proud and strong I will forever be despite the attempts to destroy the diversity of Our

My Soul in the Wind

Heavenly Father's Black family tree.

I now accept that there are those whose minds and hearts will never be free. But I will not continue to duck and dodge the "goliath" sword of internal or Xternal hatred and bigotry.

Through the years I've learned that sadness and anger turned inward will cause the human heart to drown in an ocean of tears – battered, bruised, and then broken it will, one day, attack…and finally collect on the untold years of unpaid arrears.

I am a Black Woman…one of God's brightest "shining stars" who now accepts that only He can remove the pain and erase the stain left behind by slavery's deep-rooted internal scars.

It's a sad fact, but a fact nonetheless, that there are those who will live with their pain strapped tightly to their chests…until death-do-they-part, because they'll never allow God to remove the block from their badly misused and abused human hearts.

The pervasive tactics of that wicked slave-master, Willie Lynch, has really worked well. He has gotten millions of God's people to join him in hell. He's even transformed many Black folks into bigots and snobs. But this is one Black Woman whose life this subliminal evil will not rob.

There are those who claim to fight for those who are oppressed, but secretly, even some of them wear Willie's vest – using their lips like modern-day whips…Xpecting nor wanting anything more than a Black woman who's willing to shimmy and shake her hips.

I am a Black Woman…who has struggled day-after-day just to do my best. But I will no longer struggle to pass Willie's ungodly test.

I am a Black Woman…from the soles of my feet to the tip of my head. And I refuse to lie in anyone's satanic bed. I will not be defeated, nor will I defect, for I was created to love, nurture, and protect.

I am a Black Woman…who will not accept anything less than love, honor, and respect, and; I will not live my life as a not-Black-enough "high-yellow" human reject who gets no respect.

I am a Black Woman…a sister, a mother, a friend and so much more – no longer accessible to those who will not allow God to take the long-overdue padlocks off their steel-clad doors.

I am a Black Woman…who chooses to stand forever strong…and right by my people is where I belong.

I am a Black Woman…today, tomorrow, and forever more – all the way to the center of my godly core!

Black Man

Flesh of My Flesh – Bone of My Bone…
How Do I Love Thee?

I love thee with a love that evokes a sense of harmony, balance and pride as I observe the consistency of your actions, the wonder of your wisdom, your ability to walk in the power of your divine destiny… despite the obstacles you encounter and the precision with which you execute your strategic plan for a better life for the both of us.

I love thee with the depths that no mere mortal possesses the ability to infiltrate, denigrate, manipulate or annihilate.

I love thee enough to rely on the God-given power of "discernment" to stand against the myths and misconceptions that have been calculatingly designed to minimize your worth, stifle your power and disintegrate the sanctity of our connection.

My Soul in the Wind

I love thee with a passion that supports healing from the pains of the past, the struggles of today and the uncertainty of our tomorrows.

I love thee and pray, every day, for your safety and well-being and for God's blessings that we may continue to walk together in the fullness of the light of our collective strength.

I love thee despite the fact that the world fears the divinity of your purpose, the power of your potential and the awesome reality of the man you truly are.

I love thee because time and time again you prove that despite your visible and invisible human flaws… deep within you is a heart of gold where love overflows – a love so powerful that it even transcends and surpasses human comprehension and interpretation.

I love thee even though years of secular conditioning has attempted to instill the fear of you, my Black Man, within me. But, with the help of God, I now know that it was not my own fear that I was feeding on but rather the fear others who choose to allow fear to remain a factor in their lives. Because I love thee, I choose to rebuke that fear and move forward with a greater sense of wisdom and confidence that enables me to break through every barrier that separates us.

I love thee despite the chains of oppression, the pains of separation and the weapons of segregation still aimed in our direction.

Yes, Black Man, I love thee, and I vow to never allow neither my mind nor my mouth to become weapons that penetrate, separate and ultimately break the bond of the endless love we share. My love for you is undeniable, unwavering and the faith that our love shall persevere and always prevail is unbreakable.

Together, united as one, my victorious and glorious Black Man we are strong and invincible! And I make this promise to you that no matter what weapons of psychological and physical obstacles of destruction manifest, in an attempt to tarnish and destroy our love, our family, our people – our destiny I will forever stand strong beside you, love you and honor both your needs and your guidance.

It is said that all are deserving, but not all are worthy. Today, tomorrow and every day for the rest of my life, with this pledge to you I affirm the commitment to the special love we share. I recognize and acknowledge that; indeed, you are not only deserving, but worthy. You have earned my trust and my love by not just "talking the talk," but also walking the walk. And just because you are who you are, I love thee with a depth that neither time nor evil can destroy.

My Black Man… you are an absolute glorious manifestation of God's greatest creation and a T.R.U.E. King amongst men

My Soul in the Wind

Genuine Love...

The Kind That Fits Like God's Golden Glove

Now that I've completed God's course on genuine love every day my heart soars high as the stars up above... beyond the reach of anyone toting a subliminal sword or swinging a lasso made of electric cord.

And now that I know what it feels like to be completely immersed in genuine love... I will never again engage in those subliminal head-games called "tit for tat" and "push and shove." Our Heavenly Father says that "Those are dangerous games, for genuine love never comes with internal or external boxing gloves.

Our Heavenly Father says that everyone deserves love that comes with built-in affection and absolute protection... not a daily dose of anger dispensed with an injection of a poison called instant rejection. Genuine love can't come with everything nice" as long as it's dispensed with a daily dose of satanic spice. He says that all of my children deserve love that is solid and pure for it is the only kind that will forever endure."

Our Heavenly Father warned me to always steer clear of bogus love that comes in a tiny black box that's filled with artificial highs, repetitive lies, and fictitious alibis. For this kind of love… even when new makes the heart sing songs that are solemn and blue. And when the heart can no longer sigh or cry anymore, it eventually shuts its open door – giving up on the concept of "love forever more."

Our Heavenly Father says we must never accept love that doesn't fly as free as a dove or sit as high as the moon up above. For anything less will always be nothing more than an imitation of love served with a side-dish called "chronic misery.

It took some time for me to change my internal channel from the secular dial. But now that I have, I plan to stay much longer than just awhile. For if a man is deserving of this Godly Woman's hand, he won't be marching to the tune of Willie Lynch's satanic band or toting a bucket of worthless sand expecting me to dwell in his hell located in the middle of his barren land.

Because our Father is oh so good to me, He has helped me to understand that love has the power to help even the blind to see the visibilities. Genuine Love our Father says will make every toe curl… but not for a woman with the mind of a little girl seeking it from a man whose psyche is held captive within the darkness of the devil's world.

So, until Mr. Right awakens from the night, God's making sure I remain in his ever-present sight. Our Heavenly Father says that if you want to experience love that will forever flow free, stay away from anyone who's love is a total mystery or you will end up facing a repeat of history… fooled by that same rotten fruit from that ominous tree that caused Adam and Eve to pay the ultimate fee.

Our Heavenly Father's message is oh so clear and never again will I live in wonder and fear.

My Soul in the Wind

With God on my side I will always know just what to say when crossing the path of any man who thinks I'm an easy lay. "Oh no… I'm getting my virtuous rear out of here. I refuse to shed another tear or live the rest of my life living in struggle and strife.

Now as I wait for the one who is my eternal love, I will continue to keep in mind that he will never be late for God has already designed a glorious fate for all those who are willing to wait for just the right mate who will come complete with Genuine love… the kind that fits like God's Golden Glove!

My Soul in the Wind

Joyful Bee Publishing LLC

Joyful Bee Publishing is committed to helping aspiring authors publish their work. We believe that it is important to build a brand that represents passionate individuals who have come together with the goal of succeeding at educating others with stories of trials and victories. Joyful Bee Publishing is looking for authors of all capabilities to join our growing team.

Submit Your Unpublished Work Today!

Joyfulbeepublishing@gmail.com

My Soul in the Wind

ance